2009

Poetry and Stories

by
6th grade students of
Fairfield Middle School

1st WORLD
LIBRARY
Literary Society

2009

Poetry and Stories

by 6th grade students of Fairfield Middle School

© 1st World Library - Literary Society, 2009
P. O. Box 2211, Fairfield, Iowa 52556
• Tel: 641-209-5000 • Fax: 641-209-3001
• Web: www.1stworldlibrary.com

First Edition

LCCN: 2009936288

SoftCover ISBN: 978-1-4218-9126-2
HardCover ISBN: 978-1-4218-9125-5
eBook ISBN: 978-1-4218-9127-9

Foreword

The art of instruction does not come from the act of verbally spilling out obtained knowledge, hoping that someone will catch enough to impact them in some way. Learning, in the same sense, can not be truly obtained through passive actions. To truly instruct and learn, those involved must be engaged and stimulated by what surrounds them and engrossed in the task at hand. An understanding and trust must be developed between an instructor and student so there is a level of teacher/learner in one hand and a feeling of mutual respect in the other.

Poetry is one of the most simplistic, but yet complex, expressions of instruction and learning. On the surface it appears as if one only needs a pencil, a paper, and a direction to take their thoughts with poetry. But if one delves deeper, you find that there is a much more complicated world. An instructor must be able to create an environment where students feel safe to express their feelings and reveal parts of their lives to those around them. Thoughts, emotions and actions may be expressed through poetry that students have never shared with others. Vulnerability, toughness, hope and despair can all be intertwined into an expression of one's self through minimal use of the written word. If an instructor and students can become absorbed in the process, something magical can result from their efforts.

1

The ability to organize one's thoughts, harness the emotions, and simplify the expression into a few words is no easy task at all. The confidence to share that task takes even more courage as it reveals a piece of each author. In the following, you will find poetry written by the 6th graders at Fairfield Middle School. It is the hope of the students and instructor that you find as many magical moments reading their poetry as they did creating the pieces found in this book.

Mike Dailey
Middle School Principal
Fairfield Community School District

Introduction

The poems and stories you are about to read were written and selected by sixth graders of the Fairfield Middle School in Iowa. These eleven- and twelve-year-olds were exposed to a wide variety of writing throughout the year. During our Poetry Unit, students read, chanted, sang, acted-out, interpreted, memorized, and recited poems from famous authors. They also learned how to write many different types of poems, including Japanese tanka, haiku and magazine haiku, acrostic, bio, cinquain, color poems, concrete, couplets, diamanté, holiday poems, limericks, ocean research, and title down poems. The poems in this book are the culmination of what they learned. Some are funny, clever, creative, and silly, while others are serious or sad; yet all convey the thoughts and emotions of these young, budding writers. The stories in this book were sometimes inspired by a story prompt, or from a journal entry; but mainly they come from their creative imaginations. I'm proud of their work and willingness to share this personal side of themselves with others. Happy reading!

Ann Gookin,
6th Grade Language Arts Teacher
Fairfield Middle School

3

Haiku (hi'koo) Poetry

A traditional Japanese verse, written in 17 syllables
divided into three unrhymed lines made up of
five, seven, and five syllables, often on the
subject of nature or the seasons.

Snowflakes

Falling from the sky
Crystal-like flowers up high
Drifting down slowly.

Alexis Ring

Bald Eagle

Flying in the sky
The heart of America
Majestic and strong.

Gareth West

Snails

Snails live in a pond
They slowly crawl in their shells
They heard me coming.

Gina Buelow

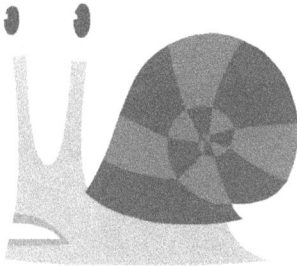

Deer

Deer are very cool
They can run very quickly
They are brown and white.

Kyle Sanders

Baseball

Let's hit a homer.
Albert Pujols get a hit,
Now steal some bases.

Alex Christensen

Flowers

Pretty flowers there,
Yellow, purple, blue, and red
In big and small groups.

Madison Aplara

Pink Flower

There you are so pink
State flower of Iowa
Growing in the ditch.

Amanda Elkins

Prom Dress

Different colors
So very pretty to see
On the big dance floor.

Jolea Burkhart

Yummy!

I like cookie dough
It is a big mess to eat
But it is so good!

Jolea Burkhart

In Your Face

How good does it taste?
Well, anyway it feels wet
Yeah, I bet it does.

Gannon Haile

Wolves

They howl every night
Wolves are so interesting
My sister loves wolves!

Kylie Roemen

Fun Outside

Outside in nature
Having fun is what I like
So much to do there.

Sidney Adam

Bright Star

Up in the bright sky
Are these shining white small stars
That look down on us.

Madison Mineart

Through the Hill

Coming off the bridge
By the mountainous hillside
Two blue engines race.

Trent Taglauer

Annoying Flies

Flies are annoying
I hate it when they bug me
I wish they would go.

Dalton McCarroll

Giraffe

Tall and very thin
Lots of brown spots all over
Six feet tall when born.

Hannah Morgan

The Playing Dog

The playing dog likes
To play poker and always
Wins for a dog treat.

Ulen Chavez

Shoes

Shoes are so awesome
They finish a great outfit
Every single time.

Hannah Morgan

Show Off

I am the turkey
When I puff myself up, I
Am just showing off!

Madison Roberts

Magazine Haiku (hi'koo) Poetry

We put a spin on the traditional Japanese verse by adding inspirational pictures from magazines and using them as our subject.

The Window

As I see through it
I see the world as it is
Colorful and calm.

Emma Lemlin

Water

Tornadoes are cool
They are twirling and spinning
I like water spouts.

Cameron Jackson

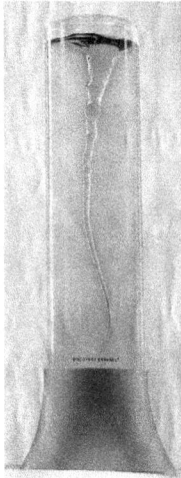

Smooth Hair

Looking at his hair
It is so smooth and shining
I'd love to touch it.

Cassandra Bran

Stuck

Flying is so fun
We are stuck on a statue
We'd rather be free.

Sidney Adam

Buzz, Buzz

I'm a pretty bee
I make delicious honey
As I work quickly.

Catherine Mwamsoyo

Baseball

Baseball is awesome
I love to hit the baseball
I hate getting out.

Cody Craff

Albert Pujols

Let's go number 5!
Here we go hitting homeruns
Let's score lots of runs!

Tanner Deao

Sour Smackers

Make your lips shiny
Be prepared to pucker up
Because it is sour!

Jasmine Elmore

Motorist

Roaming the back roads…
Going nowhere very fast
Just for a short ride.

Anthony Pruden

Motocross

He likes to race days
Sometimes you can crash and burn
But he is a pro.

Chance R. Williams

Baby Girl

Sitting on the floor
Baby girl in your blue dress
What a cute baby!

Amanda Elkins

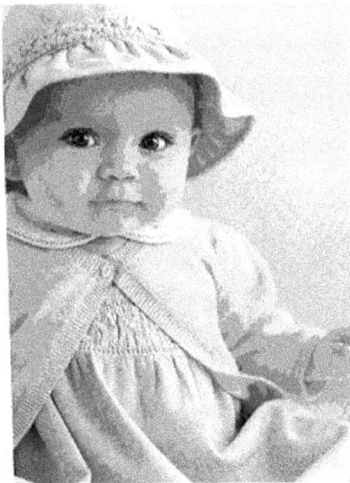

Chocolate

Chocolate is good
Sometimes it is syrupy
And you get sticky.

Leonor Gonzales

Two Bucks

Two bucks in the woods
Running like two wild ones
It's a blast of fun!

Bryana Gridley

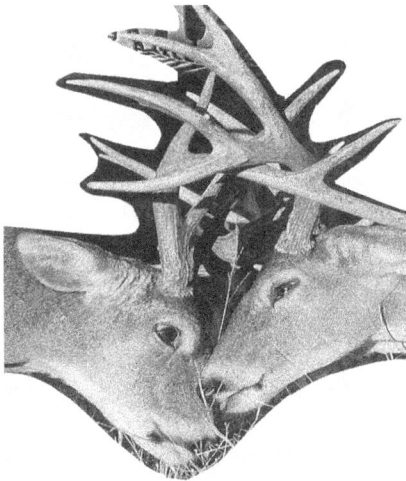

Inventor

I want to invent
And be like Jimmy Neutron
Make a robot dog.

Taylor Hudson

Number 88

High octane engine
First-ever Dale Junior bike
Number eighty-eight.

Kyle Sanders

The Fast Car

Look at this cool car
It is very fast and cool
It is so shiny!

Cody White

Concrete Poetry

A poem that visually conveys the poet's meaning
through the graphic arrangement of letters,
shapes, words, or symbols on the page.

DYNOMITE!!!

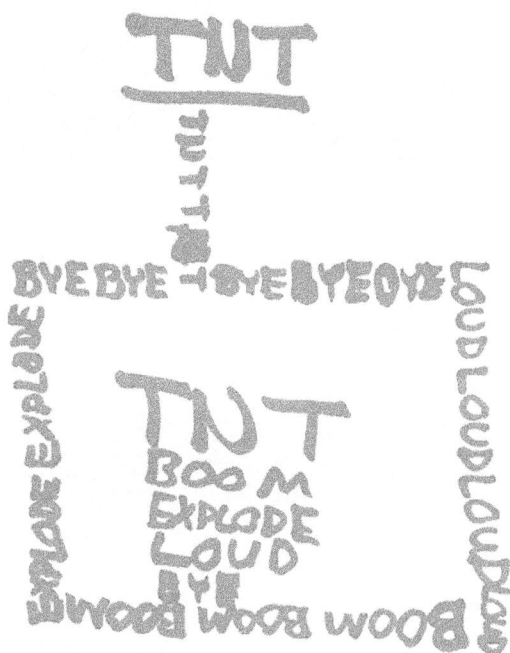

David Haynes

It Cost Me An Arm And A Leg!

Ashley Nelson

Color Poetry

A poem written about a favorite color,
using the five senses:

Taste, touch, smell, sight and sound.

This poem is packed with imagery and metaphor.

Teal

Teal is the ocean and the sky and
Smooth and wet, like water.
Teal is the taste of cotton candy.
Warm, smooth milk makes me feel teal.
Teal is the sound of water and wind.
Teal is Lake Michigan, Yosemite, and the sky.
Riding down a calm river in a small canoe is teal.
Teal is calm and serene.

Duncan Phipps

Blue

Blue is bluebells, bluebirds, and the sky.

Blue is the taste of sweet, hard,

And sticky rock candy.

Outdoors gazing at the clouds makes me feel
blue.

Blue is the sound of chirping birds

And the soft pitter patter of rain

On my windowpane.

Blue is gardens, aquariums and beaches.

A lazy summer day not doing anything is blue.

Blue is breathing in cool fresh air.

Tracy Andermann

Green

Green is leaves and grass and prickly sharp.
Green is the taste of gum.
Getting sick makes me feel green.
Green is the sound of the rattle of leaves
And the whoosh on the grass.
Green is in a tree, on the grass, and forests.
Getting sick is green.
Green is green apples.

Anthony Pruden

Blue

Blue is sky and ocean
And smooth.
Blue is the taste of winter gum.
Eating a blueberry snowcone
Makes me feel blue.
Blue is the sound of waves
And breezy.
Blue is Chicago, Wisconsin,
And an imaginary something in my room.
Lying on the ground looking at the sky with
My family is blue.
Blue is the next to the last color of the rainbow.

Cassandra Bran

Green

Green is limes and bushes and soft, cut grass.

Green is the taste of watermelon.

Climbing up in an old oak tree makes me feel
green.

Green is the sounds of dogs barking

And birds chirping.

Green is the mall, Mrs. Gookin's classroom,

And the Corn Palace in South Dakota.

Playing HyVee in softball is green.

Green is key lime pie.

Danielle Smith

Pink

Pink is a Teletubby and my softball team,
And feels sticky.
Pink is the taste of strawberries with sugar.
Being happy make me feel pink.
Pink is my bedroom, Victoria's Secret,
And American Eagle.
Shopping is pink.
Pink is cotton candy.

Madison Mineart

Pink

Pink is my nails,
Bubblicious Bubblegum
And it's fluffy.
Pink is the taste of sweets.
Pink is the sound of "tink" of the heartbeat.
Pink is weddings, my room, and the mall.
Kissing is pink.
Pink is lovely.

Catherine Mwamsoyo

Diamanté
(dee-*uh*-mahn-**tey**)Poetry

Diamante is a form of unrhymed poetry,
made up of 7 lines, the shape of a diamond. It begins
and ends with nouns of opposite meaning, and is written as a
comparison. Lines 2 and 6 use adjectives to describe the nouns,
and lines 3 and 5 use action verbs. The middle line 4 is the
magical line, where the subject gradually transforms
from one meaning to another.

Snowboarding
Cold, fun
Ramping, jumping, landing
Mountains, X- games, *pool*, *Olympics*
Diving, flipping, moving
Warm, wet
Swimming

Adam Parcell

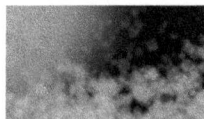

Lava
Orange, black
Burning, flaming, flowing
Magma, volcano, *freezer, glacier*
Freezing, crystallizing, sliding
Crystal, sparkly
Ice

Cameron Jackson

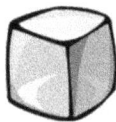

Quiet

Calm, peaceful

Whispering, sleeping, unspeaking

Parents, sisters, cousins, neighbors

Blustering, booming, yelling

Noisy, clamorous

Loud

Cody Craff

Sky
Never-ending, blue
Floating, moving, flying
Kites, balloons, *sand, dirt*
Tickling, growing, sprouting
Green, dry
Ground

Emma Lemlin

LOVE
Trust, respect
Relaxing, caring, bonding
Friend, home, *danger, bully*
Controlling, pushing, saddening
Mean, unlikeable
HATE

Hailey Coop

Cold
Chilly, cool
Shivering, freezing, sledding
Windy, ice, *sun, beach*
Sweating, swimming, surfing
Sunny, warm
Hot

Bryana Gridley

Water
Calm, reflective
Flowing, splashing, dripping
Waves, rivers, ashes, embers
Burning, heating, exploding
Destructive, hot
Fire

Ian Gottshall

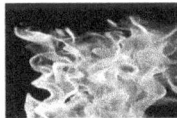

River
Fast, cold,
Diving, growing, loaded,
Des Moines, creek, swimmers, lake
Dammed, settling, cleared,
Deeper, warm
Pond

J.T. Tedrow

Inside
Cold, dark
Reading, writing, cooking
Rooms, pencils, *ocean, trees*
Playing, skating, running
Sunny, hot
Outside

Jolea Burkhart

Iowa
Perfect, reliable
Educating, honored, loving
Football, wrestling, losers, animals
Frustrating, irritating, annoying
Horrible, worthless
Iowa State

Landen Greiner

Alive
Warm, bright
Living, breathing, moving
People, animals, mummies, skeletons
Rotting, no heartbeat, no seeing
Cold, pale
Dead

Paris Bickham

Spring
Humid, hot
Playing, skateboarding, planting
Hills, leaves, *snow, mountains*
Skiing, sledding, ice skating
Cold, windy
Fall

Robbie Kloski

Pixies
Small, beautiful
Flying, jumping, spinning
Fairy, midget, ogres, gremlins
Running, walking, grunting
Ugly, smelly
Trolls

Sarah Wallingford

Life
Colorful, happy
Exciting, living, existing
You, me, *Elvis, relatives*
Depressing, sickened, crying
Black, underground
Death

Sierra Simmons

Spring
Wet, warm
Growing, living, looking
Babies, plants, football, basketball
Dying, chilling, falling
Yellow, brown
Fall

Taylor Hudson

Outside
Nice, green
Running, jumping, skipping
Playground, grass, bed, television
Eating, watching, sleeping
Crowded, small
Inside

Ulen Chavez

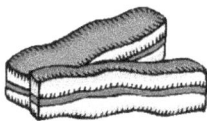

Bacon
Wrinkly, yummy
Sizzling, stinking, molding
Pigs, grease, *humongous, old*
Growing, falling, rooting
Mossy, leafy
Trees

Ryan Laughlin

Reality
Real, non-fiction
Skating, shooting, reading
Mountains, chocolate, *trolls, flying monkeys*
Sword-fighting, flying, reviving
Fake, fiction
Fantasy

Evan Wood

Tanka (täng'*kuh*) Poetry

A Japanese poem consisting of 31 syllables in 5
lines, with 5 syllables in the first and third lines,
and 7 in the others.

Autumn

Falling down from trees
Shriveled up leaves coming down
Coming down slowly
Colorful leaves everywhere
Bringing out the best of all.

Alexis Ring

Glacier

Cold, unforgiving,
Freezing all in sight, water
Especially so,
Grinding, crushing, frigidy,
Destruction is all that's left.

Duncan Phipps

Painful Snow

Snowing so hard out
I can't even see the lawn
It's killing the grass
When I try to shovel it,
It seems to snow much harder.

Bryce Lunsford

The Night Sky

Shiny stars twinkle
The moonlight shimmers brightly
Northern lights are bright
I may see the Milky Way
Maybe I will tomorrow.

Gannon Haile

Summer

When the sun blazes
Heat flowing off from the sun
Swimming in the pool
Laying out in the hot sun
Enjoying it while it lasts.

Emma Lemlin

Autumn Breeze

Swinging through the clouds
Whirling up the orange leaves
Blowing all the clouds
Man, I cannot wait to feel
The warm and crisp autumn breeze!

Trent Taglauer

Winter

Snow covers the ground
It is blowing everywhere
Snow is very white
It's fun to play in the snow
Snow's very cold and icy.

Kylie Roemen

Winter

Winter sun hiding
Super cool dude snowboarding
Carries the snowboard
All the way up the steep hill
'Til he snowboards down the hill.

Logan Fleeman

Track

When the guns go off
I run as fast as I can
Running out of breath
Wondering if I'm in first
While crossing the finish line.

Madison Mineart

Camping

Sleeping in a tent
Underneath the night time sky
The night is calm and
Still, as the night lingers on
Soon it will be morning time.

Meghan Shelangoski

The Skier

A skier skiing
Down a steep, mountainous slope,
Leaving a long trail
In the white, powdery snow,
Hoping not to lose balance.

Ian Gottshall

Acrostic (*uh*-kraw'-stik) Poetry

A short poem in which the initial letters of the lines,
taken in order, spell a person's name.

David Stephanie

Different
Adventurer
Very good at eating food fast
I like burgers
Demanding

Slow
Tidy
Excited always
Positive
Happy
Apples are my favorite
Nice
Inviting
Enchanting

David Stephanie

Ocean Poetry

Our sixth graders at F.M.S. study an oceanography
unit in science where they research and find ten
facts about a living animal or plant from the ocean.
In language arts class, students use their research
facts to create a poem.

The Very Tubby Seal

I am a tubby gray seal.
When my pups are born, they are very chubby.

I love to eat crustaceans like shrimp, and lobster.

I can weigh up to 880 pounds.
I like to live on big sand mounds.

When I eat, I eat 11 pounds a day.
I like this water, I think I'll stay.

Diving is my best talent.
I can dive to 475 feet.

In my kind of water, I don't like heat.

How I move is swim and scoot.
But when it comes to me, I sure don't hoot.

My name means 'hook-nosed sea pig'.
I am very big.

I can grow to almost 10 feet long.
And at night I like to sing a song.

So bye now, and have a nice day.
Remember not to pollute my water and I will stay.

Ashley Nelson

The Green Giant

I am the Giant Green Sea Anemone
My body is sticky and soft.
I am a wonderful and beautiful green color
And I like to cling to rocks.

I live along the Pacific Coast
And I like to eat passing prey.
I do not tolerate polluted water
Not a single second of the day.

I have a few different enemies like
Sea spiders and the Wentletrap snail.
If you touch my long tentacles,
You might let out a big wail.

That is the poison being ejected
But don't you go and worry,
The poison is normally harmless to humans
So please don't leave in a hurry.

I am green because algae lives with me
They make a home in my tissues,
But that's okay, 'cause they make a good snack
And the never cause me issues.

I can grow to 10 inches in diameter.
I am the largest anemone on the coast.
I can eat a Giant Crab and spit out the shell
In 15 minutes at the most.

I don't really move I just sit there,
And let my tentacles sway.
I hope you enjoyed learning about me,
And I hope to see you again someday!

Ashlee Hardeman

The Fish with the Lion's Mane

I am the Lion's Mane Jellyfish.
I glide through the water with gentle ease,
A small, yummy fish is sure to please.

My tentacles are orange and red,
I have a glob of jelly for a head.

I may sting and I may bite,
The pain may reach an extreme height.

I am the largest of my kind,
Try to hurt me, and you'll be in a bind.

Planktonic crustations and fish eggs are my
specialty,
Sea turtles, sea birds, and large fish are my enemies.

I prefer to swim in cold waters,
I sway near the surface with my 310 daughters.

Autumn Taylor

The Clowny Clown Fish

I'm orange, black, and white,
I live in the coral and I do not bite.

I'm found in the Western Pacific.

Males have only one white bar,
I use coral to blend in, in case of cars.

I eat plants, not animals.

I can have one hundred babies at once,
Hopefully, I won't lose them all and be a klutz.

I can have up to three white bars,
If I were a female.

Cody White

The Sandy Swimmer

I am the biggest of them all,
For I get my name from my rubbery tough hull.

I've only been seen off of Newfoundland,
Norway, and New Zealand.

I only come on dry land
When I'm laying down my 85 eggs.

I am very hard to see
With my dark brown shell.

I love to snack
On the jellyfish pack,
Or maybe some krill,
Or even some shrill.

But when I'm floating silently,
They sometimes sneak behind me:

The dreaded plastic BAGS!!!!!!

I am protected by law,
So you can't eat me with your jaw.

When I'm swimming silently,
I may get stung by electrifying tentacles.

I love to swim
For I am the Leather Back Turtle!

Dakota Webber

Giant Worm

I'm skinny and long.

I can grow to be 8 feet long and I'm red and white.

I live next to smokers, 2,500 meters deep in the sea.

I don't eat much, but bacteria and plankton would be best.

I have a nickname, Raffia pachyptila.

I have very few predators.

I'm unique because I'm the longest-living neocolonial invertebrate.

Dalton McCarroll

Hammer Head Horror

My head is big.
    Half the size of my body, too.
        I swing my head, so I can see you.

I love sting rays, they are really good,
    Some of us grow to be 19.5 feet, wish I could.

I swim with friends, and I swim with schools,
    Now isn't that cool!

You can't see me, even right in front of you.
    My head is flat, but is also fat.

I swim to the bottom to get the rays,
    But when I get there, I dig for my prey.

Since my head is flat, it's hard for me to see,
    When I get there, if you're scared you might pee.

I'm known to kill you,
    But if you hide, I'm sure to find.

David Haynes

King of the Dinosaurs

I am the Plesiosaurus.

I lived way back when dinosaurs ruled the earth

And man was not made yet.

I lived in the great big seas.

I dove and flew through the oceans waves,

With my great big flippers,

And long neck to see.

I feed on belemnites and fishies in the sea.

I am related to the elasamasaurus

Who is a close brother to me.

I use my flippers as paddles to propel me
through the currents.

I use my neck as a rudder to twist and turn in the
sea.

I swim far down in the ocean depths.

And wiggle and shake till I find a decent tasty
  meal.

I am no longer alive, *"because"* is the question,

For no one knows what happened to us
  dinosaurs.

But one thing's for sure, with my sharp teeth and
  big body,

That makes me the king of the dinosaurs!

Gareth West

Psychedelic

Look at me, the Psychedelic Fish!

I am plump and round with a flat face,
I bounce off the coral at an unruly pace.

My colors are white, peach, and blue,
I was just discovered, so I am new.

I live within the coral reefs,
I eat without any teeth.

Wrinkly and thick describes my skin,
I also have strange leg-like fins.

My diet is currently unknown,
I think I would rather be left alone.

Gina Buelow

Who Lives at the Bottom of the Sea?

I am a Tripod fish,
T-R-I-P-O-D,
And I live at the bottom of every sea.

Way down in the deep blue,
I eat algae and dookie which are hard to chew.

Well, I don't have a last name like Foster,
But I am named for my unusual posture.

Oh, and don't forget about my three elongated fins,
I walk around on the ground with these big thins,
They are quite sweet like spinnin' rims.

I don't have to wait for a mate,
Because I don't quite believe in fate,
I am a hermaphrodite and I can be my own date.

I may have extremely small eyes on top of my head,
But don't be frightened, I can still be your friend.

Hailey Coop

The Spike Ball

I have marble like eyes, and spikes like a porcupine.

I live in and around the coral reef.

I like to swim in the 50 foot pool,
(the shallow end).

I am a predator of oysters, clams,
and other invertebrates.

I love my look when I inflate myself
with air or water.

I am the Porcupine Fish.

J. T. Tedrow

Wonderful Whale Shark

I am the wonderful whale shark,
   I eat perfect plankton,
      Awesome anchovies, and
        Kool krill.

My eggs are the world's largest eggs,
They are 40 times bigger than a chicken's eggs.
   I always live in the tough tropical waters.
     I am the world's largest fish
       In the whole wide world.

I have a big number of tiny teeth,
   If I bite you,
      Or your arm or leg gets caught in my mouth,
       You will be badly bruised.
   My skin is gray all over with big white blotchy
spots.

   I'm so wide, I don't think I can move sideways,
So I think I am just going to stick with straight.

Jasmine Elmore

The Sideways Walker

My width is eleven inches,

And my legs grow as long as six feet.

We are also called stone crabs.

We are mostly found in Alaska, Japan, and
  Siberia.

I am mostly found in the cold seas.

I eat sea stars, urchins, clams, barnacles,

And other benthic invertebrates.

When we are living, we are purple.

When we are cooked, we turn red.

We walk sideways.

I am the King crab.

Kelsey Thacker

Spin, Spinner, Spin

As my skin glistens in the warm sun,

The grey and pink on my belly shows off.

Some of the other animals say that my jaw looks
  like a bird's,

But I say, "Look at you. You are as big as a cow
  herd!"

When I swim through the Atlantic, Indian and
  the Pacific,

Everybody watches me when I spin and do tricks.

Through the water I go,

Eating squid and small fish,

Tearing them apart with most of my conical
  teeth.

I love to play around, making my clicking noises,

We always show off, doing our sophisticated poses.

As I spin through the sunset sky,

My friends use echolocation to tell me,

"Look, there's a flying fly!"

I splish and I splash and I swim very fast,

None of my enemies can get me because I'm too
  hard to catch.

I am the Spinner Dolphin.

Leonor Gonzalez

The Ugly Coolie

I am the Coolie Loach.
I have 3 pairs of whiskers
And 12-17 vertical dark bars.
You can find me in Southeast Asia,
Sumatra, Singapore, Western Malaysia,
Java, Borneo, and Thailand.
I munch on tropical fish flakes.
Worms are my favorite,
But I will eat anything that settles at the bottom.
Prickly Eye, Kulie Loach, Giant Coolie Loach,
And Leopard Loach are all of my nicknames.
I can get up to 4 inches long!
I swim at the bottom of the deep blue sea,
So no one can see me!!

Mackenzie McClure

The Puffy Ball of Kindness

I am the shy Red Sea Puffer Fish!

My black mask flies across my eyes,
My mouth is curvy like a beak.

I dream of being with a team of frozen preparations in which is my treat.
Although I am a carnivore, I am on a diet.

I seem to be cute and cuddly,
But my skin is prickly with scaly scales everywhere.

I try my best to beat the rest from others above and down.
So I hide in my lovely home the coral in which I marvel.

I wish people would not eat me, because my
  body is not meant for somebody.

You might think "ha!" but trust me; you won't be
  alive the next time you try.

You see, I am very round as I swim around with
  my fins,

But in me is a horrible poison.

This poison covers all my organs keeping me safe
  and sound.

I am the Red Sea Puffer Fish, I mean no harm.

Please, oh please, let me be alone in my corner,
  safe and alone.

Marina Ginther

Awesome Ray

I am a spotted Eagle Ray.
I have spots on my back,
And I don't like to attack,
But when I want a snack,
I go for my favorite dish,
No, it's not fish;
It's a nice juicy mollusk.

I have to be careful,
Because I am nearly threatened.
I like to swim near the surface.
When I'm out of the water,
I make a loud sound,
It makes them want to put me back.

Down into the water I go,
I am not afraid, because I am not slow.
I am one of the few
That can pump uterine milk directly into my baby's
embryo.
When I get old, my tail falls off,
When I swim I glide through the water.

Nick Jackson

121

The Color of my Eyes is my Name

The color of my eyes is my name,
Which is not a shame.

I have three vertical lines on my sides,
11 full inches is my size, but
My brothers may get bigger than me.

We always are very territorial.

When I hunt for something good to eat,
What catches my eyes first, isn't meat,
Though little creatures can't be beat.

I eat anemone,
Which helps me raise my family.

I live in the tropics,
Where it is hot.

When I have babies, I lay eggs.
Then I guard them every day.

Though we are pretty, we are VERY aggressive,
Don't you thing that's most impressive?

I am a Maroon Clownfish!

Rebekah Carter

Not So Coral

I am Fire Coral.

I am yellow, and I will sting you if you come near.

I look like petrified wood.

The tropical waters are my beloved home.

My jellyfish relatives tremble with fear.

My no-food habit has driven me crazy,

While my ocean neighbors are pushing daisies.

While I am just sitting doing nothing at all,

My relatives, the jellyfish, are having a ball.

While I sit here watching divers go past me,

If they swim into me, my poison wouldn't make
them happy.

Sarah Wallingford

124

The Magic Maroon

I'm the magic Maroon Clownfish.

I am the most awesome fish.

Now watch me pull a rabbit from my hat.

And then smack it with a bat.

Watch it swoosh through the ocean water.

Oops it hit an otter!

Now look at me with my soft skin.

Oh, Ow! I hit my fin!

I'm a dark maroon or black.

I can break the coral with a smack.

I move with a wiggle of my fins,

I eat plankton all day long,

And I live in the bubbletip anemone.

Now that was me, the Magic Maroon.

Now I hope to see you again soon!

Ryan Laughlin

Wide Open

My name's the Sand Tiger Shark,
I don't live in the dark.
Find me, I live in the sand by the coast,
Yes! It's time for a roast.
I like squid, small sharks, lobsters, and crab,
But I'm really small, so that's a drab.

      I'm only ten and a half feet long.
      I swim with my mouth wide open,
      When I'm a baby I have brown spots.
      As I am an adult,
      It's not my fault.
      But I'm a third place medal color on top,
      Yet pale on my bottom.

Never forget about me,
My name's the Sand Tiger Shark.

Sierra Simmons

The Teeny Weenie Ghost

Hello, I'm in my cave, let me come out,
Now I must go scurry about.
    It's breakfast time!
    It's breakfast time!
I'll find some fish,
    I will turn it into a very fancy dish.
I know, I know, am hard to see, because I am so
clear,
    I know, I know, I am so small, I am so hard to
        hear.
I am so cool, I have six legs.
    I really like to crawl,
It looks like I'm flying.
    I live in caves, near the shore in any ocean.
I am common in the tropics.
    I am different in some ways, like my big one arm.
        I really must go, sorry, but I am tired.
        I am a ghost shrimp.

Ulen Chavez

My Life as a Haddock

I'm the haddock.

I'm a popular food dude.

I weigh up to 30 pounds,

And I live about 600 feet down.

I'm greenish brown, and a little tan.

I'm smaller than cod,

But bigger that tomcod.

I'm very odd.

I swim with my fins.

I live in the cold European waters.

I mature at 3 or 4 years old.

I eat mollusks, crabs, and worms.

Zane Richmond

Ancient Assassin

I am the Ancient Assassin.

I glide silently through the water unnoticed.

I eat small fish and crabs,

And my scales feel rough like scabs.

I sometimes like to lie on the Indonesian coast,

However, I like the deep the most.

I'm over 400 million years old,

But I still look the same.

I'm a Coelacanth and that's my name.

Evan Wood

The Drunk Driver

I am the endangered Nautilus,
I swim 100 meters, backwards.
In my awesome small herds,
Look at my racing stripes.
And my tentacle-like pipes.
My family is the *Nautilidae,*
And when I swim, you'll see I glide.
I live in the Pacific,
With my tentacles, I'll kick.

Alex Christensen

Title Down Poetry

A poem that vertically tells a story,
using the letters of its title.

Teach

Treating
Everybody with respect
Always
Calling on students
Having troubles.

Alexis McElroy

Flute

Fluttering a
Lullaby
Until
The sound
Echoes.

Alexis Ring

Kitten

Kind and cute
I see you
There on
The floor,
Even though you are hiding
Now there you go running away.

Amanda Elkins

135

John Deere

Jeff is my dad and he rides
On
His John Deere and says
Nothing runs like a Deere!

Do other tractors run like a Deere? NO!
Everyday my dad tells me that.
Especially the
Red ones, they are never
Ever good tractors!

Ashlee Hardeman

JOHN DEERE

Void

Very dark and
Ominous, like the blackness
In space, which makes you
Delirious and crazy!

Duncan Phipps

Family

Forever to be together
And never to be broken
Moments to be memories that
I will never forget.
Love is a key word and
You will always be remembered.

Gannon Haile

138

Dog

Darn animals jumping on their
Owners and then
Getting into trouble.

Hannah Morgan

Hitting

High
In
The air
To the fence
Incoming runners
Not
Going to get out.

Harley Cook

Softball

Smacking the ball
Over the
Fence, hoping
To win, running the
Bases
As fast as I can,
Letting the scores get higher
Laughing because we won the game.

Harley Cook

Dog

Dangerous and

Over-calmed when other dogs come
  and

Go they bark at people, too.

Keven Beamish

Light

Light
Illuminating everything is
Great, but you
Have to admit, it's annoying when
  you're
Trying to sleep.

Ian Gottshall

143

Bacon

Bacon is good
At
Christmas time and
On
Nachos.

Josh Broeg

Brother

Bothering me all the time,
Reminding me he is
Older,
Telling me what to do,
Helping me with my homework,
Entertaining me with his jokes and
Reminding me how lucky I am.

Madison Aplara

Golf

Guys and gals
Of all ages
Love this game
Forever and ever.

Michael Hemm

Brothers

Blake is his name. He loves

Running

Over

The grass around the

House.

Every time he shouts out, "Loser,"
  and

Runs, he

Slips & slides in the mud, rolling &
  laughing with a big smile.

Marina Ginther

Ill

I hate being sick because it's
Lousy and
Loaded with pain!

Nicholas Jackson

Softball

Some
Of us people
Fall in love with
The game where neon
Balls fly
All around,
Lifting and
Laying about.

Sierra Simmons

Football

Far down the field
On the field go post is an
Orange pad that says
"Trojans" on it as a
Ball flies through the goal,
All the people cheer very
Loudly as the Trojan
Legends score.

Tanner Deao

Stories

Stow away

To write,

Of course dont forget your imagina-
tion;

Riding a horse

Inside a cave, it's

Easy to write,

So easy.

Tracy Andermann

Trains

Transporting
Really large
Amounts of coal
In the USA;
Never short and
Sometimes late.

Trent Taglauer

Guitars

Guitars are awesome. They
Undulate sound waves for miles
  around, but
I 'll probably
Tear everyone's eardrums in half.
A wesome sounds will come from it,
Rendering everything quiet, when I
  break a
String.

Zach Smith

Pasture Poems Inspired By Robert Frost

Famous American poet, Robert Frost, (1874 -1963), author of "The Pasture," inspired us when we read his old-fashioned poem. The following poems, written by our sixth graders, are updated interpretations of Frost's "Pasture" poem.

The Pasture

I'm going out to clean the pasture spring;

I'll only stop to rake the leaves away

(And wait to watch the water clear, I may):

I shan't be gone long.—You come too.

I'm going out to fetch the little calf

That's standing by the mother. It's so young,

It totters when she licks it with her tongue.

I shan't be gone long.—You come too.

Robert Frost

My Pasture Poem

I'm going out to Ohio
To see my newborn niece
And take her a blanket of fleece
I shan't be gone long.—You come too.

I'm going out to ride in a car
I'm going to read my book
It's so good, I think I'm hooked
I shan't be gone long.—You come too.

Ashlee Hardeman

157

My Pasture Poem

I'm going out to buy a new guitar:

I don't know which to buy; I hope I don't
make a mistake

My annoying little sister, I'll be sure not to
take

I shan't be gone long. — You come too.

I'm going out to take over the world:

I'll make everybody give me presents and
gifts

I'll destroy all vegetables and make schools
myths

I shan't be gone long. — You come too.

Austin Corrick

My Pasture Poem

I'm going out to the park
It's going to be fun playing ball
Well, it's raining 'cause it's fall
I shan't be gone long.—You come too.

I'm going out to the movies
I'm going to be there at night
At least we aren't in the light
I shan't be gone long.—You come too.

Chris Manning

My Pasture Poem

I'm going out to play catch
I'll only stop to get a drink
After the game, I'll probably stink
I shan't be gone long.—You come too.

I'm going out to shoot hoops
I'll only stop to take a break
And when I'm home, I'll probably ache
I shan't be gone long.—You come too.

Dalton McCarroll

My Pasture Poem

I'm going out to ride my bike
I'll ride it around the pond
Hoping to take my sister, Skyler, so we can
    bond
I shan't be gone long.—You come too.

I'm going out to the park today:
I'll take my dog for a walk
I'll bring my best friend so we can talk
I shan't be gone long.—You come too.

Kylie Roemen

161

My Pasture Poem

I'm going out to shop at the mall

I'm going to shop 'till I drop

And go wave at a mall cop

I shan't be long gone.—You come too.

I'm going out to the Sweet Spot

I'm going out to get some Eskimo Kisses

Yeah, it's an ice cream with chocolaty crisp-
    ness

I shan't be gone long.—You come too.

Leonor Gonzalez

My Pasture Poem

I'm going out to ride my four-wheeler
I love to go really fast
Oh, no! I almost crashed
I shan't be gone long.—You come too.

Madison Roberts

My Pasture Poem

I'm going out to the mall to shop
I'll be sure to stop in every store
It will be very fun, I'm sure
I shan't be gone long—you come too.

After I'm done, I'll stop for a pizza
I'll invite my friends on this trip
I'll be sure to leave a big tip
I shan't be gone long—you come too.

Meghan Shelangoski

My Pasture Poem

I'm going out to fetch my cat:
It got mad at me and spat
It ran to the barn and there it sat:
I shan't be gone long,—you come too.

I'm going out to fetch my dog:
It chased my cat around the barn
I now need to fetch both, darn!
I shan't be gone long,—you come too.

Tracy Andermann

165

Bio Poetry
(bi'o)=life

A poem about one's life.

My Bio Poem

Ashley

Active, quiet, smart, talkative

Oldest child of Shawn and Heather

Lover of animals, softball, math

Who feels happy, bored, hungry

Who needs an i-Pod, a pool, a trampoline

Who fears being home alone, the dark, the
neighbor two houses down

Who would like to see The Statue of Liberty,
St. Louis Arch, Disney World

Resident of Lockridge; Willow Blvd.

Nelson

Ashley Nelson

169

My Bio Poem

Douglas

Fun, active, nice, dangerous

Oldest brother of Delanie and Cian

Lover of football, orange juice, strawberries

Who feels happy, sad, curious

Who needs a new dirt bike, football, video
game

Who fears getting hurt, being late, car acci-
dents

Who would like to see Alaska, go to the
Super Bowl, Italy

Resident of Fairfield; E. Adams

Bonnett

Douglas Bonnett

My Bio Poem

Alexis

Smart, outgoing, friendly, exciting

Oldest child of Morgen and Emma

Lover of animals, softball, and four-wheeling

Who feels tired when school gets out, happy
playing sports, glad when we get a
longer weekend

Who needs a new cell phone, Internet,
clothes

Who fears walking home when there is a
murderer in Fairfield, watching really
scary movies, and getting grounded

Who would like my mom to win the lottery,
keep my sister from wearing my clothes,
the Fairfield Trojans to do better than they
did last year

Resident of Fairfield; West Washington

McElroy

Alexis McElroy

171

My Bio Poem

Andrew

Nice, cool, awesome, busy

Youngest child of Melinda and Frank

Lover of pizza, frogs, spiders

Who feels tired, happy, crazy

Who needs my own computer, new bike,
moped

Who fears bridges, rivers, trains

Who would like to see Europe, Australia,
Boston Red Sox win World Series

Resident of Fairfield; West Carpenter

Chatfield

Andrew Chatfield

My Bio Poem

Jasmine

Sweet, funny, outgoing, nice

Oldest sister of Ashlyn and Carson

Lover of pizza, softball, volleyball

Who feels happy on Fridays, hungry, tired at
home

Who needs a cell phone, laptop, new room

Who fears sharks, snakes, jellyfish

Who would like to see Hawaii, France,
Germany

Resident of Libertyville; W. Maple

Elmore

Jasmine Elmore

My Bio Poem

Kilee

Sweet, lovable, pretty, huggable

Daughter of Sergio and Abbey Scharf

Lover of cats, dogs, turtles

Who feels tired after school, playing, and
biking

Who needs my own money, room and a pink
bed set

Who fears crossing streets on a bike, getting
F's, and dogs chasing me

Who would like to see Hawaii, under the sea,
and getting on a boat

Resident of Fairfield; Carpenter Street

Williams

Kilee Williams

My Bio Poem

Rebekah

Caring, kind, friendly, Christian

Daughter of Linda S. Brown and Ron A.
  Carter

Lover of food, people, church

Who feels kind, nice, sleepy

Who needs a computer in my room, a cell
  phone, new clothes

Who fears reading, shopping for shoes, dogs
  getting in my face

Who would like to see my mom, my dad,
  and my grandpa

Resident of Libertyville; Douds Road

Carter

Rebekah Carter

My Bio Poem

Trent

Kind, helpful, collector, cattle shower

Oldest child of Mark & Laura

Lover of trains, pasta, swimming

Who feels relieved after school, good when swimming, energized when running

Who needs a four- wheeler, an allowance, goats

Who fears heights, bullies, darkness

Who would like to see Mom win $34,000,000, my brother to leave me alone, get a UTV

Resident of Brighton; Willow Blvd.

Taglauer

Trent Taglauer

Limerick (lim'er-ik) Poetry

A humorous, five-lined poem with an a-a-b-b-a
rhythm & rhyme, using one couplet and one triplet.

Knowledge Vs. My Sister

Knowledge is what my sister lacks
I think I'll tell her some facts
    When I walked up to her she said,
    "I'm tired, I'm gonna go to bed."
I decided to give her a few smacks.

Clara Kelley

Things Found
Poetry

Things Found In An Attic

A dead mouse
Dusty pictures
Cobwebs
Black bats
A dusty old wooden bat
Dead spiders
A dusty old rocking chair
Very dusty boxes
Dusty pink insulation
As well as a trunk with Grandma's treasures

Adam Parcell

Cody White

Anthony Pruden

183

What I Did On A Rainy Day

Mom made a sigh,

As we waited for it to pass by,

With the thunder,

And the lumber outside,

I started to tremble,

I was scared of the rumble and crash,

But instead,

Dad said,

"LET'S PLAY LIMBO!!"

So I sat by the window,

Waiting my turn and

I learned I'm not scared,

Of the rumble and crash!

Rebekah Carter

Kilee Williams

184

Things Found Out of a Semi Truck Window

I see, I see, I see,
I see birds fly past me.
In the shining night,
My lights shine bright.
Every time I look down,
I frown,
Because there's road kill.
My job takes me many places.
As I see a wall of green,
It's very easy to be seen.
As I look out the cab window,
I see the tops
Of lots
Of cars, street signs, and more!!

Paris Bickham

Meghan Shelangoski

Madison Aplara

Taylor Hudson

185

Miscellaneous
Poetry

Sleigh Bells

Novelty manger
Odd snowmen
Wishes coming true
Believing in Santa
Apple pie baking
Little children sitting on Santa's lap
Lit up Christmas trees
Family Guy marathons
Illuminated houses
Glowing garland
Holiday music
Tinsel around a tree

Landen Greiner

189

The Many Colors of Christmas

I like the colors of Christmas!
Red for Santa's sleigh
Green for the tree
Brown for the reindeer
Gold for the angel
White for the snow
I like the colors of Christmas!

Douglas Bonnett

Christmas Time

Christmas!

I *see* presents
I *smell* food
I *hear* bells
I *taste* mashed potatoes
I *touch* toys

Douglas Bonnett

191

Merry Christmas!

I like the colors of Christmas.
Red for Santa's suit
Green as the Christmas tree
Blue as the blubs on the tree
Silver as the bright lights
Gold as the tree top angel
I like the colors of Christmas.

Danielle Smith

Jolly Old St. Nick

Joyful
Old
Loveable
Likes kids
Yells "Ho, ho, ho!"

Overweight
Loves to fly
Down on houses

Snow on ground
Toys

Nice
It's just what I wanted
Cold
Kicks back

Danielle Smith

193

STORIES By

6th Grade Students of

The Fairfield Middle School

2009

Pearl Harbor

It was the morning of December 7th, 1941. My fellow classmates and I decided to become army nurses, so we had gone to Oahu, Hawaii. Our house was only a one-mile walk from Pearl Harbor.

We were outside watching the sunrise, when suddenly a fleet of fighter airplanes flew by. We all thought it was the B16 California's coming in, but they were flying unfamiliarly low. A couple minutes later, the earth started to shake.

Our neighbor screamed from the yard next to us, "BOMB!"

We ran to the clearing where we could see the harbor perfectly. We saw the worst thing in the world. Our neighbor was right. A bomb had hit the U.S.S. Oklahoma. The massive battleship was slowly tilting over. Men were sliding and trying to grasp the chains on the ship.

We just stood there, frozen. I tried to move my shoes, but they felt glued. My mouth was so wide, you could hide in it.

I finally got myself to say, "Everyone to the hospital."

I knew today was not going to be slow. After five

197

minutes, 20 guys had come in. I couldn't believe my eyes. Horror was everywhere around me. Someone had informed me that the U.S.S. Missouri and Oklahoma had all been blown in half. Soon after, news caught up to us.

"We have come to inform you that the U.S.S. Arizona was hit. As you know, it had many men on it. We are looking for survivors. Please make room for these men," said General Opal.

General Opal was right, and 200 came in. Screams of terror were everywhere. It was my job to mark who would survive and who wouldn't. I hated my job. Many times I had to lie, so they wouldn't think about dying.

I would say, "It will be all right," or "It's okay," when I knew it wasn't.

"We need anyone who has total control over their limbs," wailed Officer Colbalt. He had told me that men were trapped in the hull of the Arizona. With only minutes left, 20 guys had fit the bill.

"We need more men!" yelled Officer Colbalt.

"What if I go?" I exclaimed, not believing what I was saying.

"You? You're just a *woman*," laughed Officer Colbalt and two other officers.

"So? I've seen worse than what's out there. I've had to make the decision of who lived and who died. So don't give me the speech on '*you're just a woman*' because I'm a bigger man than *you'll* ever be." I couldn't believe what I was saying. Part of me wanted-ed to say more, but I just kept quiet.

"Fine. You can come, but I warn you, it's bad out there," Officer Colbalt told me.

"Okay, but don't ever say *'I'm just a woman'*," I explained to him.

He was so right. It was bad. The harbor was full of bodies. Many were still alive, starting to get tired from treading water. When we got close to the battleships, you could hear them in there, banging on the sides of the ship.

Half of us went to the harbor; others went to the air strip. Planes were also blown to pieces; others only bumped. Innocent people were also there.

Many people died that day. So we went to Japan and destroyed it. The World War II was our shortest war. I will remember that day forever.

Some Interesting Facts

1. When the U.S.S. Arizona went down, it took one million gallons of gas with it. Today it leaks between a quart and a cup.

2. Pearl Harbor is still an active military base.

3. The U.S.S. Arizona was never decommissioned.

4. Margret Truman commissioned the U.S.S. Missouri on January 21, 1940. She died on January 21, 2008.

Kotie Webber

Redhawk

Prologue

"Gareth, oh my gosh! Gareth, don't look! Go to your room, please, Gareth! You shouldn't see this."

Those are the words Gareth West, a four-year-old boy, heard on September 11, 2001, when a plane crashed into the World Trade Center, killing so many. That day changed his life. He saw what evil could happen in the world; what horrifying things can happen; how much killing can happen. That day scarred Gareth for his whole life. He was not different, by looking at him. You would say he looked like any other four-year-old boy, but because of that day, something in Gareth said, *'if no one right now could stop it, who could?'* That day, Gareth vowed to make sure that could never happen again, one step at a time.

Chapter One

The Opportunity

Now Gareth is 12 years old and has been training ever since that day. He has trained to be stronger every day. He has now moved to crime-filled Fairtown. He has trained himself hard till he could not anymore, and he's done this everyday. He learned many techniques and was able to piece together one of his own fighting styles. He attends Fairtown Junior High. He has made many friends, and you would never guess he would have this secret ambition. Gareth has an especially close friend named Ian, who is, technically, a genius and a talented inventor. He's richer than Mitus. But even though his life was good, there was always something missing... his sense of justice, his compelling feeling to make a difference.

RIIINNNNNNGGH!

"Class dismissed," yelled the voice of one of Fairtown Junior High's homeroom teacher.

A cocky voice called, "Hey, Gareth."

A quick shove from behind gave Gareth a stumble.

"Leave me alone, Austin."

"Hey, kids, get going!" the janitor yelled.

"Well, see ya later," Austin sneered.

Thirty minutes later, Gareth was walking home. He saw an old man standing there on the street, asking for money.

"Please," he croaked.

Gareth felt a five dollar bill in his pocket. Fingering it, he decides.

"Here," he says in a kind tone, as he gave the man the bill.

"Thank you, young sir! May I ask your name?"

Grudgingly Gareth replies, "It's Gareth."

"Well, Gareth, I must repay you somehow," the old man pries.

"No," Gareth said, "that won't be necessary," as he eases back.

"No," the old man said, "I insist, follow me."

So, thinking the withered old man could not be harmful and feeling kind of warmth and wisdom in the man, Gareth cautiously follows the old man deep through a grassy park, until they get to a type of hut.

The man turned and with a new strength and pride, almost glowing, the man asks, "Now, Gareth, what would you like?"

TO BE CONTINUED IN REDHAWK, THE NOVEL

Gareth West

The Monkey

Once upon a time there was a monkey. He was a smart monkey. He wanted clothes. The only person he knew who had material was an evil scary rabbit. He was too scared to go to the rabbit, so he decided he would get the fur from an animal. First, he went to his friend, the dragon, and got a sewing machine. Then, he snuck up on a squirrel and chopped off some fur from his tail. It wasn't enough to make any clothes, so he made the squirrel some socks and the squirrel forgave him for stealing fur.

Next, he went to the lion and said, "May I have the fur from your mane?"

"NO!" said the lion. "I would look like a girl."

He thought that maybe he could trick the rabbit. He went to the dragon and got a rabbit costume and a map to the rabbit's den. He walked through Firecracker Forest and over Peacock Hill. There, the monkey stood, looking like a rabbit halfway up Dead Mountain. He saw the rabbit's cave and started to climb the mountain. He got all the way up and he saw the rabbit. Since the monkey looked like a rabbit, the other rabbit invited him in.

"What do you want?" said the rabbit.

"I want you to help me get fur from an animal that doesn't need it," said the monkey.

"An elephant," said the rabbit.

"Elephants don't have fur!" exclaimed the monkey.

"Are you doubting my skills? Go to Fluff Hill!" rabbit screamed.

"Ok," whispered the monkey.

The monkey started running for his life. The monkey got out his phone and called the dragon for a map to Fluff Hill. When the map arrived, he started on his journey. He went through Smiley Star Town. He had to go over a rainbow and at the end he found gold. Then he came to the biggest hill he had ever seen. He got on his scuba gear and swam through the air. Up, up, up, and POP! He couldn't go any farther up. He landed halfway up the hill. He saw a bunch of fluff on the ground. He went to pick it up.

It said, "Hey, stop that! Use scissors and get it off me please," pleaded the thing.

"Oops," called the monkey. "What are you?"

"An elephant," explained the thing.

The monkey dumped out his gold and cut the fluff off the elephant and put it in the pot. The monkey went all the way back to his tree house and made himself clothes. Since the elephant had no fluff, he became a swimmer and won the Olympics. The monkey moved to L.A. and became a movie producer, made millions, and became famous. The dragon made a batch of cookies. They all lived happily ever after.

Sidney Adam

A Day at Six Flags

When I lived in Dallas, Texas, we lived twenty to thirty minutes away from Six Flags Amusement Park. We went there almost every weekend because we had season passes, so that was cool.

I used to love to go to Six Flags because they have so many rides. I can't even name them all. My favorites were probably the Cobra, the Pirate Ship, and The Texas Giant. The Cobra is a mix of a water slide and a roller coaster. It is a fun and fast ride.

The Pirate Ship is a big ship and it swings back and forth. Everytime we went to Six Flags, we would go on the Sombrero, The Texas Giant, Pirate Ship, Judge Roy Scream, and sometimes the Log Ride.

One time we went at night on Halloween and we were watching some people dressed up, dancing to Thriller. One of the people there came behind my mom and wasn't breathing and scared her. It was funny.

We went on a lot of rides on Halloween. It was dark out, but they had a lot of lights on so it was really fun. I hope we can go to Six Flags again sometime.

Adam Parcell

The Super Bowl Game

The day of the Super Bowl game, my dad came and got Abbey and me at our grandma and grandpa's house. After that, we went home for an hour. My mom was home with the flu, so my dad said, "Let's go so we don't miss the game."

We got in the car and left. When we were halfway into Fairfield, the fire department was going crazy. We drove on and when we got to my grandma's, my aunt was there with my cousins, Dylan and Destiny. A few minutes later, my other aunt Sherry and my cousin Matt came. After everyone was there, we ordered pizza. When the pizza came, we ate and watched the game.

My grandma said, "We should never buy from there again. It's too spicy!"

My aunt said, "It was good."

My cousin Austin cheered, "The Steelers are going to crush the Cardinals!"

When the game was almost over, Austin did a front flip off my grandma's couch. Then we all left and Austin was happy that the Steelers won!

Bryana Gridley

My Life, My World

Hi! My name is Catherine. I was born at St. Francis Hospital in Dar es Salaam, Tanzania. I arrived three weeks late. I'm the first-born child of Godfrey and Monica Mwamsoyo. I have two brothers, Cuthbert, a first grade 7-year-old, and Collin, a 16-month-old baby. I'm a 6th grader at Fairfield Middle School.

I haven't always lived at Fairfield. When I was five, I moved from Dar es Salaam to Des Moines, Iowa. We moved because my dad wanted to go to college at Maharishi University in Fairfield in 2001, while my mom was pregnant.

The night before we left, when I was five, I had an accident with my leg. We don't know what happened; it just started bleeding really bad. So my mom rushed me to the hospital and I got a cast and a wheelchair. Then the next day we left. We had to take two planes to get to America and one to Des Moines.

When we were getting on our third plane, my leg began to hurt again. I was in major pain and I started crying, and so did Cuthbert, after seeing me cry. The pilot made us get off the plane because I was too sick to move. Then my leg kept on bleeding and I was yelling and crying, so they called an ambulance and I got off the plane at Atlanta, Georgia. They took me by ambulance to the Atlanta Hospital, where I took some meds and stayed there for two days.

While we were at the hospital, my mom called my dad and told him what happened and that we would be delayed. I felt sorry for my brother because he had to spend his first birthday at the hospital and it wasn't his fault. After two days, my mom, brother and I flew to Des Moines, where later I had more problems with my leg. I had surgery and discovered that I had two broken bones and I got stitches and had to use crutches for about two months. So we lived in Des Moines for awhile, and then we moved to Fairfield, and have been living here ever since.

In the summer of 2006, we went to San Antonio, Texas, for a week by train which was really fun. We visited some close friends and went swimming in the Gulf of Mexico.

During the summer of 2007, I joined softball and have been playing ever since. It's my favorite sport, next to basketball. During fourth and fifth grades, I received a lot of art awards. In fourth grade, my picture was selected to be in the Iowa traveling show, where it traveled to schools all over Iowa. I also got my first perfect attendance award in fifth grade.

In the summer of 2007, my brother Collin was born, and then the following summer, I went to Camp L-Kee-Ta for five days.

This past August, I started middle school. I'm in band and play the clarinet. My favorite book is *Taking Care of Moses* and my favorite actress and singers are

Keke Palmer & Raven Symone. My favorite show is "True Jackson VP" and "iCarly". When I grow up, I want to go to George Town University on a softball-basketball scholarship to study to be a doctor.

Catherine Mwamsoyo

Embarrassing Accident

When I was in 5th grade, we were practicing a tornado drill and I ripped my pants, but I didn't know 'til I went to the bathroom later. Luckily, nobody noticed until I changed clothes. I had to wait in the office for 30 minutes. It was right before lunch. It was so embarrassing, but my mom and I had a good laugh about it!

Cody White

Time's Up...

BOOM!!!

Dirt, blood, and limbs of the fallen soldiers fly into the air.

"MEMINGER!!!" yelled Lieutenant Parker.

"Yes, sir?" I shouted.

"Get in that hole before you get shot."

"YES, SIR," I yelled.

I didn't want to get shot. Especially by those dirty, stinking Nazis. If I didn't get blown up, I knew I was going to get shot.

"Marshalls? Are you ok?"

"Yes, sir, I'm fine. Bleeding a lot, but fine," yelled Marshalls. "I was shot in my left shoulder. I can't shoot anymore, sir."

"Then find Copeland and have him call in an air strike," Lieutenant Parker yelled.

BOOM!!! Another bomb exploded.

"Sir, Copeland is dead. But I can call the air strike," Marshalls stated. Marshalls didn't know how to call the strike, all he knew was that after he did, he had to run far, and fast.

"Marshalls to base, Marshalls to base, do you read me?"

"You have been acknowledged, what do you need?" the base commander said.

"Sir, we are in the downtown district of Berlin and we need an air strike," Marshalls yelled.

"We have advised the Air Force and they are on their way," the commander stated.

"Thank you, sir," Marshalls yelled. "Lieutenant, we have the Air Force en route and they will be here in a matter of minutes."

He knew that he had to make it to the base, but did he have time?

"Marshalls, Meminger, Lee, Henagar, all of you get back to the bunker, and that's an order," Lieutenant yelled. All of them scrambled out of the trenches and ran for their lives. Marshalls was shot as soon as he was out of the trench, and the Lieutenant shot the Nazi who did it. His blood spattered everywhere. The Lieutenant saw the men run, but he stayed in the trenches, providing as much cover as he could.

"I'll see you in Hell, Nazis!!" yelled the Lieutenant. He threw a grenade.

BOOM!!! It blew up three Nazis; and then another grenade.

BOOM!!!

"*Herr, dass Mann dabei ist, uns alle zu töten,*" yelled one of the Nazis.

"Sir, that man is going to kill us all."

"Finden Sie gut eine Weise, diesen Mann zu töten," yelled the Nazi Commander. *"Well, find a way to kill that man."*

"Die you stinking Nazis!!" yelled Lieutenant, and he threw another grenade.

BOOM!!! Another grenade exploded. It killed four Nazis, including the Commander.

"Ok, I think that was the last Nazi," muttered the Lieutenant. He stood up. Big mistake.

"Sterben Sie Sie amerikanisches Schwein," yelled a Nazi sniper, *"Die you American swine."*

BANG!!! It was a one shot kill. Lieutenant Parker's blood splattered everywhere.

"Heil Hitler," yelled the sniper.

Only two men made it back to that bunker, both thought to be the luckiest person alive. They never knew that Lieutenant Parker was killed. But his time was up. As was Copeland's and Marshall's. Time's up…

"Sir, we are en route to Berlin…Sir?" said the pilot. He was unaware that they had been out of the battle.

"STRAHLEN!!" yelled one of the remaining Nazis," *Kommen Sie Im Graben,"* *"JETS!! Get In The Trenches!"* All of the remaining Nazis dove into the trenches.

BOOM!!! BOOM!!! BOOM!!! Bombs from the jets exploded over the trenches.

214

"Decken Sie ihre Köpfe," yelled a Nazi, *"Cover your heads!"* All of the Nazis put on their helmets and covered their heads with their guns. The mud piled into the trenches. The Nazis were getting buried alive.

"Bitte lässt Herr uns leben," muttered one of the Nazis, *"Please, lord, let us live."* All of the Nazis bent over and prayed for their safety. Only for a minute though.

"Sterben Sie Sie amerikanisches Schwein," yelled the Nazis, *"Die you American swine!"*

BANG!!! BANG!!! The Nazis shot down a P-51 Mustang, the best American fighter jet. With the Mustang, were three P-41 Warhawks.

"Die Amerikaner müssen sterben," yelled a Nazi pilot, *"The Americans must die."* The Nazis came in with five Heinkel Salamanders.

BOOM!!! An American pilot shot down a Salamander. The wreckage exploded, sending molten steel down onto the Nazis and the dead American soldiers.

"Lee, you have a Salamander on your 20," said Colonel Sanders.

"I don't see it, Taylor, all I see is you and Kloski," said Lee.

BOOM!!! Sanders got shot down, he plummeted into the trench.

Evan Wood

215

My Big Trip to Florida

One winter my mom, dad, grandma, and I went to Florida. At first, I thought it would be boring. However, when we got to the hotel, it was awesome. There was a hot tub, a flat screen TV, a big bed, and leather couches. When we were there, I had my first Shirley Temple. It was nice getting out of Iowa. We went by airplane. My ears popped, so a nice lady gave me some gum. It worked. We went to Disney World and Sea World. At Disney World, we rode roller coasters, water slides, tea cups from "Beauty and the Beast." I also got to be in the parade and met Cinderella and Bell. It was gnarly, dude. I got sunburned, but that didn't stop me from having fun. I also met Mickey Mouse and got his autograph. I went into the hot tub. It was nice.

The next day, we went to Sea World. We saw Flipper and his brother. They are dolphins. I got a penny and put it in a machine and it flattened it and put an imprint of Flipper on it. I got to touch a dolphin. It was cool!! I've loved dolphins ever since.

I loved that trip so much that we're going back. It was fun! I can't wait to go again and again. I wish I could live there, but I can't. I was really hot when we left. It was like 110 degrees outside. I made a mistake and wore a skirt and a tank top back to Iowa. I was freezing on the way home, but I still had fun.

Kilee Williams

Four Little Girls

It was about 4:30 on a Wednesday. A group of boys were walking through the park, when one of them tripped over an uneven patch of dirt. They all got down on their hands and knees to look closer. Then Mark, the oldest, said he would go get some shovels so they could see what was underneath the dirt.

When he got back, the boys started to dig. After about five minutes of digging, Jake hit something. Then Nick, John, Tyler and Mark hit something, too. Nick got down and brushed off the dirt only to find a decently-sized big box. The boys lifted the box out of the hole and tried to open it, but it wouldn't move. Then Tyler noticed that it was locked. The boys carried the box to Mark's car and drove back to John's house to try to open it with tools.

When the boys got there, it was almost dark outside. They carried the box into John's garage. Nick went over to the tool bench and got some bolt cutters. After Nick, John, Jake, and Tyler tried to open it, and had no luck, Mark tried. He struggled at first, but finally got the lock off.

The boys were not scared to open the box, but John's little sister, Mary, came out to the garage. They had to wait until she left. Mary went and sat down right beside John. He told her to leave, but she said she didn't have to.

"You're not the boss of me!"

John picked her up and put her in the house and locked the door.

The boys finally opened the box. Inside were four bags that were sort of decayed. The boys were about to open the bags, when John's mother told the boys it was time to go. The boys planned to meet back at John's house the next day.

While John waited for his friends to come back, he thought about opening the bags, but decided to wait until his friends got there. When his friends finally showed up, they went over to the box and took the bags out. When Tyler picked up a heavy bag, the bag broke and a little girl fell to the ground. Tyler jumped back. The other boys were too afraid to open the bags now.

They went to John's mom and told her everything that had happened. She asked to see the bodies just to see if they were fake. When she looked, they weren't.

They went to the police and told them what had happened, too. They said that they would like to see the bodies. They asked a lot of questions, like *How long ago did you find the bodies? How many were there? Are there just bones? Was there flesh still on the bodies?*

The boys and the police went back and got the box and put the bodies in it. Then the police took the bodies to the police station to be carefully examined.

The boys were asked even more questions!

The police came back from the examining room and said there was a body in each of the bags. They could not find any fingerprints or locks of hair that didn't belong to the girls. They said the girls had been missing for about two months. Their parents would be glad they had been found, but disappointed that they were dead.

The police searched the bodies again and again but never found any evidence. The murderer was never caught.

Madison Roberts

My Little Pal

I can feel his fur. It is as soft as cotton. I see his eyes sparkle like marbles. I see the orange, as bright as the sun, and the white as white as snow. This creature is not just a hamster, it is my pal!!

I always loved how he ran on my hands. He thought it was a treadmill.

He always ran in his wheel that went around and around. He thought it was a bed. He would carry food and bedding and put it in the wheel. He always begged for some more food. I gave him food anyway because he looked so cute.

Everyone knows hamsters cannot live forever, but he was the oldest hamster in the world to me.

After school, I gladly headed home. My mom said that I should hold Sunny Sundae because he did not look well. When I looked at him, he was not moving. We put him safely in his cage and looked at him. He breathed every so often. Suddenly I realized what I had to do. I told my mom to let him go. She went in the other room and called the vet. I heard her say how much it was to put Sunny Sundae to sleep. I could not bear it. I held my tears, but they slipped right out. Hot tears rained down my cheeks. I petted him and fed him water. I looked at him I said, "I love you" and "You will be ok."

Soon it was time to go. I put him in a small cage and we headed to the vet. I petted him the whole time. A nurse took me and my brother and mom. We went in a room and waited with Sunny Sundae. I cried and cried, but I knew this was right. I knew he was going to heaven and he would even meet his friends Alvin, and Oreo. Maybe he will go with his cage, too.

The nurse came in and talked peacefully. She talked about my hamster and his cage and that I was doing the right thing. She said he was handsome and she said he must have been loved well. I petted Sunny Sundae one last time and watched him go. It felt like I was losing everything.

In the car, I thought how Sunny Sundae first started. I was glad I still had his cage, but I just wished he was still in the towel. I wished I was bringing him back home.

I remember why his name was Sunny Sundae. *Sunny*, because he was orange as the sun and loved to be by the sun, and *Sundae*, because he looked like ice cream. Blake, my brother, even gave him a nickname **Sunny D.** I loved that name. I always called him that, but now he is Sunny Sundae.

I love Sunny Sundae so much! I will never forget him! I promised him I would not forget.

Marina Ginther

My Special Person, Audry

I have a lot of special people in my life. But one stands out to me. She's always been there for me if I'm sad, confused, excited, happy, or anything in between. If I'm depressed about myself, she always tells me positive things like, "Sierra, you're beautiful and wonderful." If she wasn't in my life I would be lost. I call her every night and we just talk for hours, never running out of things to say.

We also have so many memories together, like the time we drove across the entire state of Iowa, or when we sat in her bedroom till six in the morning talking and playing games. Also, on New Year's Eve every year, we stay up all night and call everyone, screaming at the top of our lungs at midnight, even my mom! I remember her putting peanut butter in my hair and staying at my house alone all day, too. We have too many memories to even remember!

This girl is beautiful in every way. You should meet her because she is just amazing. This is to my very special person, Audry.

Sierra Simmons

223

My Summer Break Adventure
In St. Louis

This summer I took an adventure to St. Louis, Missouri, in July with my mom, and my brother. It was a lot of fun. We left our house at about 6:00 A.M. on July 19th, 2008. It took about four hours to get from our house to the Missouri border. As we were driving, we watched videos and played games on my laptop.

When we got to the border, we started to see all kinds of road work and a lot of firework stores. We saw a lot of deer. One of the deer ran out in front of our car.

When we finally got to St. Louis, it was rush hour. It took a lot of patience. Finally, we got to the Metro Link Train Station and we got on an electric powered unit. We rode a long way. We stopped at Grand Rail Station and got off of the train going south and got on the train going north.

The next day we rode the Metro Link to the Arch. The Arch was very tall. We went into the underground waiting area and museum. There, we bought tickets for a trip to the top of the Arch. After an hour, we got on the lift to the top. It is like a theme park ride and an elevator put together. It takes about four minutes to get the top.

Once at the top, we got to walk around. It wasn't that scary. It was really cool to see all of the land from the top of the Arch. When it was time to leave, we got back in our car and left the top of the Arch. It only takes about three minutes to get to the bottom.

After the Arch, we got on the Metro Link Train again and went looking around the city. We saw a lot of cool things. My favorite thing was the BNSF Train going through St. Louis.

The next day we went to Six Flags Theme Park. It was a lot of fun. We went to the rollercoaster Batman. My favorite ride was the Mine Train Coaster. After lunch, we went to the water park. The funnel ride was my favorite water slide. After the water park, we went to the Lady Anta Bella concert. My brother and I went to the concert and halfway through, we went to the Mine Train Coaster. When we were done at Six Flags, we went to the restaurant, Applebee's. It was delicious. I had some mini bacon burgers.

The next day we went to the Science Center. It was so factual. I learned about electricity and computer codes. The Space Shuttle Technology Museum was cool, too. I saw an elevator as a space shuttle. I also drove a model plane.

After the Science Center, we went home. It was a long trip home. My brother and I wanted some fireworks, but we got there too late. We were half asleep when we got to the Iowa border, but we had fun.

Trent Taglauer

225

Alex and One Very, Very Super, Horrible, Very Stinking, Bad Day

One day, Alex Rodriguez, (no, not A-Rod), woke up on his birthday and said, "This'll be the best day ever!" For his birthday, his parents were buying him a moped for when he turned 14.

"Alex, time for breakfast," his mom yelled from downstairs.

"Coming!" he answered.

He got dressed really fast and took the stairs two at a time. It was Wednesday, French toast day, his favorite food. He cleared all of the steps, except the last one. He tripped and fell, landed on his face, and got a bloody nose.

"OW!" he screamed.

"Oh, my goodness! Honey, are you all right?" his mom asked.

"Ha ha!" laughed his evil little sister.

"It's not funny!"

"Yes it is! Ha ha-ha-ha…" she burst out laughing.

When he was all ready for school, cleaned off and fed, he left his house only to see his bus already at the stop, waiting for him. Once he got on, everyone started laughing! Then he realized he forgot his pants!!!

He went back inside, put them on, and ran back out to the bus, only to find it halfway down the street already. He ran inside again, found his mom, and asked her, "Mom, will you give me a ride to school?"

"No, honey, I have to go to work."

"Dang it!"

So, he walked. When he was halfway there, it started to storm.

"Oh, come on," he shouted. He sprinted the rest of the way.

When he got to school, it was halfway through first period. It was his tenth tardy, so he got suspended. He was furious. He had to walk in the rain all over again.

When he got home, he turned on the TV and saw the tornado warning signal on. He started to hear the tornado sirens go off. He figured it was just a test, so he stayed upstairs. *But it was raining,* so... he thought. The tornado hit his house, not doing much damage, but sucking up only his TV, his X-box 360, his bed, and his PS3. It also hit him in the back of the head with a vase.

When his parents got home with the moped, they came inside to find Alex sitting on the floor of his room, holding his head and saying, "Ow! Ow! Ow!"

"What happened to all of your stuff?" his dad asked.

He told them. They were surprised nothing else was missing. But you should have seen the look on their faces when he told them he got suspended! They were so mad, they took the moped back!

"No! No! Please don't take the moped back," wailed Alex, dragging on his mom's ankle.

"No. You got suspended, so no moped for you."

"You can buy one yourself once you get enough money, but you're sure as heck not getting one from us," added his dad.

Alex's "best day ever" ended up being his worst day ever. He got suspended, didn't get a moped, broke his nose, and lost all of his video games, but hey... he didn't have to go to school!

Zach Smith

The Tunnel

It all started out when Rachel asked to go for a walk. I had insisted on having Rachel over to spend the night. Mom had agreed, and so had Rachel's mom. She came Friday to Saturday. It was after lunch and Rachel wanted to do something other than stay inside.

"Let's go for a walk!" she said.

"Okay," I replied.

"I want to go, let me go, too!" my little brother whined. He was such a pest.

"He'll follow us anywhere!" I whispered to Rachel.

"Yeah," said Rachel. "Let's ditch him!"

We got our shoes on and went outside. Tommy followed. I looked at my watch. It had a built in compass, flashlight, safety pin, and a rope that could come out and retract. It was twelve o'clock.

"Hey, Tommy!" I said. "Isn't it just about time for *Barney*?"

"Oh, yeah. See you later!" Tommy said. He turned and ran back into the house.

"Come on!" I hissed. "Run!"

We ran to the bushes behind the house. I heard the door open and Tommy's voice.

"Hey! Where'd you go? It was only time for that show about the ducks!"

I heard him walk around the house. He didn't see us. He went inside.

"Phew!" Rachel said. "That was a close call!"

We walked back to the clearing behind the house. We separated, Rachel about ten feet away from me. All of the sudden, she called my name.

"Katie! Look what I found!" she exclaimed.

I ran over to her.

"Look at this huge sparkling rock! I want it, I want it, I want it, I want it!"

"Keep your pants on," I said. "I'm getting tired anyway. Pick it up and let's leave."

She bent down and tried to pull it out, but it was stuck. She tried to push it the other way, but it wouldn't budge.

"Help me get it out!" Rachel cried in frustration.

I stooped down, and together we managed to pull it out. Rachel picked up the rock and started to walk away. I looked where the rock had been. There was a hole! There was a rope ladder leading up to the ground.

"Rachel!" I cried. "Come here, fast!"

She came walking back lugging the rock.

"Katie, did you really have to make me walk all the way back, hauling this huge heavy rock just to...." She stopped short, staring at the hole.

"I'm going in," I said. Carefully I stepped into the hole, feet on the ladder, climbing down. Rachel followed slowly. We got to the bottom. It was pitch black.

"Hah!" Rachel said. "It's dark. We have to go back up."

I looked at her with a smirk on my face and flipped the light on my watch. She glared at me. We walked through the cold, dark tunnels, my brown shoulder-length hair bouncing against my back. Rachel, with her red curls stuck to her neck, was practically clinging to me in fright. There was a thundering roar, getting closer as we walked. It was getting brighter. We walked into this huge scenery-like plant place with a huge waterfall. Rachel and I stared at each other, in total amazement.

"It could our secret hiding spot!" Rachel exclaimed. "Let's go back."

We walked to the tunnel entrance and I tried to turn the flashlight on. Nothing happened. I tried again. The batteries were dead.

"Hurry up and turn the light on! I want to go back out," Rachel said.

"The batteries are dead!" I said strongly, trying to hide the tremble in my voice that shook me. "The ladder was on this side, so we can feel our way out!"

We found the right side of the wall and started to

leave. I was in the lead. I stumbled over rocks and scraped my palms on the wall, desperate to get out. I saw a light. We had reached the ladder. As I gripped the ladder, halfway up, I felt it sagging against my weight. I heard a tearing sound and then I was on the ground.

"Katie!" Rachel shrieked in horror. I opened my eyes and tried to stand up. My right foot hurt a lot and so did my head. I collapsed in pain.

"I've got to get you out of here," Rachel said. She stared at my watch. "I've got it!" she said excitedly.

She gently took my watch off my arm and took out the rope. Then, she started climbing the wall, holding the ladder. She found foot holes in the wall. I bit my lip when she looked like she was going to fall. She cut some rope off, using my safety pin to cut with, and tied the rope ladder together. Then she climbed down and tied the rest of the rope to my waist. She climbed up and pulled the rope. I hung there and let her pull me up. When I opened my eyes, I could taste fresh air. Rachel grabbed my arms and pulled me out of the hole. Then, she carefully pushed the sparkly rock over the hole. When we got home, I went to the hospital. I had a broken leg and was lucky I didn't break my neck.

As for the tunnel, we never went down to it again.

Tracy Andermann

See 1stWorld Books at:

www.1stWorldPublishing.com

See our classic collection at:

www.1stWorldLibrary.com

www.ingramcontent.com/pod-product-compliance
Lightning Source LLC
Chambersburg PA
CBHW022015090426

42739CB00006BA/150